The Tech Entrepreneur's Financial Playbook

Winning Plays for Forming, Financing
& Operating Tech Companies

Second Edition

Evan Rogoff

BALBOA.
PRESS
A DIVISION OF HAY HOUSE

Balboa Press books may be ordered through booksellers or by contacting:

Balboa Press
A Division of Hay House
1663 Liberty Drive
Bloomington, IN 47403
www.balboapress.com
1 (877) 407-4847

Print information available on the last page.

ISBN: 978-1-9822-1680-1 (sc)
ISBN: 978-1-9822-1681-8 (hc)
ISBN: 978-1-9822-1684-9 (e)

Library of Congress Control Number: 2018913849

Balboa Press rev. date: 11/29/2018

"Concise, well organized and easy to read!… this is what a starting entrepreneur needs."

-Venkata, PhD & Entrepreneur

Contents

Foreword

As a management professor, entrepreneur and former CEO of several technology companies, I've been a part of many startup and growing businesses. Like myself, so many of my students and fellow entrepreneurs are terrific at spotting market opportunities and developing products to serve new markets. We obsess over our products and customers and try to avoid complicated back-office functions like finance, human resources and governance.

"The Tech Entrepreneur's Financial Playbook" is a fantastic guide and must-read for first-time entrepreneurs, to get their new business started the right foot. Evan's advice is presented in an easy-to-read, step-by-step format to quickly and inexpensively make decisions about complex topics. His guidance simplifies decisions that lawyers and accountants can overcomplicate.

I recommend this book to all of my MBA students and all the first-time entrepreneurs who I advise. Evan's advice saves time and money, keeps you out of trouble with the tax authorities and sets your business up for success with venture capital investors and acquirers.

Gregory Quinet

Associate Professor & Assistant Director of the Michael A. Level School of Management at Kennesaw State University

Introduction

When an entrepreneur starts a business, his or her focus is on developing a product or service to sell to customers, and then on landing the initial customers. Off the radar for most entrepreneurs are mundane tasks relating to accounting, finance, governance and human resources. These tasks are often ignored by small companies that don't know what to do and are confused by complex requirements from various jurisdictions.

Service providers (lawyers, accountants and insurance brokers) are more than happy to elaborate on risks, using fear to prove their own knowledge and drive revenues for themselves. Professional fees for a cash-strapped, pre-revenue, pre-product business can total tens of thousands of dollars initially just to set up a business entity, money a startup just doesn't have. Overthinking these issues at can lead to unnecessary complexity, which requires ongoing costly and burdensome maintenance throughout the company's life, while failing to meet the entrepreneur's real needs.

Entrepreneurs often fumble through these issues when trying to formalize the company's structure. Or a jack-of-all-trades office admin may be tasked to address these topics without any training or guidance in these areas and without the judgment of how to balance risks and rewards of noncompliance. So, too often simple administrative tasks go ignored.

Yet these roles are critical to every company large and small. Without back office tasks being performed regularly and accurately, a company will be swamped during due diligence from an investor or acquirer. Or a surprise state tax audit could turn ugly. Also, management won't understand how the company is performing or how much capital is available to reinvest in growth. But these responsibilities can be addressed simply and at a low cost in any small technology business.

Built on three decades of entrepreneurship and honed by experience working with dozens of entrepreneurs, this text guides entrepreneurs on best practices that I've developed for the necessary back office functions of a technology business. This text includes steps to effectively implement simple procedures so that finance and administration doesn't impede the company's growth or valuation.

Formation: Tips on Choosing the Best Operating Entity

This chapter on Formation addresses the following topics:

- Choice of entity
- State of jurisdiction
- Dun & Bradstreet
- Other formation issues

When starting and forming a company, most businesses have little or no capital. Entrepreneurs have little desire to invest the time or money to get it right at this stage. However, a few decisions at the formation stage are critical to meeting the company's long-term objectives and can be done quickly and with modest cost.

Key decisions to be made around company formation include:

Choice of entity: LLC vs. Corporation

The first step in forming a business is to set up the company's legal structure. There are a myriad of choices when considering the structure of a new company including: sole proprietorship, general or limited partnership, limited liability partnership (LLP), limited liability limited partnership (LLLP), limited liability company (LLC), single member limited liability company (SMLLC), C-corporation, S-corporation, professional corporation (PC), etc.

Many factors will determine which of the above forms of legal structure is most appropriate for the business. A good corporate lawyer can help navigate through these complexities. A quick online search will give plenty of information about the choice of entity; likely far too much information to be helpful. Most startup technology companies choose between LLC and C-corporation.

Both LLC and C-corporation are common, well-understood legal entities. Several big differences between an LLC and a C-corporation are tax-related:

- Income taxes:
  An LLC is a "flow through" entity for U.S. tax purposes, meaning the company does not pay corporate income taxes, rather all profits and losses flow automatically to the company's owners. This is true whether or not the company distributes profits to the owners in cash. The flow through nature of an LLC minimizes the double-taxation risk of C-corporations but can complicate tax reporting if a company has many owners.
  A C-corporation will owe taxes on its profits, and in addition owners will owe taxes on any funds distributed by the company (from dividends for example). This is commonly referred to as the double-taxation problem.

- Governance:

  An LLC structure can be very simple and provide a lot of flexibility to the owners to structure voting, fiduciary responsibilities, distribution of proceeds, etc. A C-corporation on the other hand is more structured and must abide by various state laws regarding governance and treatment of owners.

- Exit transaction:

  Because of the double-taxation burden, C-corporations upon exit generally must sell stock in a transaction with an acquirer, since the sale of assets may result in double-taxation. An LLC has greater flexibility to minimize taxes in an exit transaction which can increase exit valuation for sellers. See Playbook 10 for more information on exit transactions.

Companies will often start as an LLC since LLC formation fast and inexpensive, while at the same time providing tax benefits to initial owners if the company will initially be unprofitable (as most new companies are).

Sophisticated institutional investors (angels and venture capital firms) will mandate a company be a C-corporation. Lawyers can convert a company from LLC to C-corporation if needed upon the initial investment. Or, if a company intends to quickly raise outside capital, simply form the company as a C-corporation initially.

Other corporate structures such as S-corporation (which is really just a regular corporation that elects to be taxed differently), PC, LLP, etc. are far less common, and are rarely used by startup technology companies. Use of these other forms of corporate structure would likely cause raised eyebrows from investors and other third parties.

> *Story: A digital marketing company was established as a C-corporation because the founders expected to eventually raise venture capital and assumed that these investors would require a corporate structure. Their plan was to pursue these venture investors a couple years in the future, before which the company would incur substantial losses that angel investors wanted to deduct on their personal tax returns. So, they filed an election with the IRS to treat the corporation as an S-corporation, which is unusual for tech companies and tech industry investors. Later on, when the time came to discuss investment with more sophisticated investors, most were shocked at the S-corporation election. They weren't familiar with the S-corporation tax status but had been advised to avoid companies in such a structure, which complicated the company's ability to raise venture capital.*

State of jurisdiction: Delaware vs. Local

Companies (LLCs and C-corporations) are formed under the laws of one of the U.S. states, not under any specific Federal law. A company can choose which state's laws to incorporate under, the choice being either (i) choosing to use the home state where the company's primary office will be located or (ii) choosing a state that is more beneficial to the company.

The simplest way to form a company is to do so in the local home state. Local lawyers will be familiar with the state's laws and formation process. The downside is that some states are not as business friendly as others, so choosing another state may be beneficial long term to the business.

Delaware is considered generally among the most business-friendly states and its courts have seen significant corporation litigation over the years, so there's a clear track record of how its courts will rule in important governance matters. But while Delaware may offer benefits, having a foreign state of jurisdiction requires a local presence in that state. Third parties (called registered agents) will, for a fee, gladly provide the local presence.

Many companies will start out as a local company incorporated under the laws of their local State, since this is typically fastest and easiest.

Sophisticated investors will mandate a company be formed in Delaware. Lawyers can reestablish a company from a local to a Delaware company. Or, if a company intends to quickly raise outside capital from institutional investors, simply form the company in Delaware initially.

The company's lawyers can form the company but also much of this can be handled by a non-lawyer by going to the website of the appropriate Secretary of State, which usually has a "Corporation" division.

Paperwork required

Each state has slightly different paperwork requirements, but generally follow the following outline:

LLC's require a certificate of organization (filed with the secretary of state) and an operating agreement. Establishing bylaws is wise. Anyone obtaining an ownership interest (a.k.a. units) should purchase such ownership interest through a subscription agreement or unit purchase agreement. All such documents should be in writing and approved by the board of managers or shareholders.

C-corporations require a certificate of incorporation (filed with the secretary of state). Establishing bylaws is wise. Anyone obtaining an ownership interest (a.k.a. shares) should purchase such ownership interest through a subscription agreement or share purchase agreement. All such documents should be in writing and approved by the board of directors or shareholders.

The company's corporate lawyers can draft the appropriate paperwork for formation. Bootstrapped startups can find templates for many of these agreements online or can borrow and repurpose these agreements from other entrepreneurs. But be careful because poorly drafted documents without appropriate protections for the company and shareholders can be costly if not impossible to correct later. So usually it's best to have the startup paperwork done right the first time.

In either case once the company is formed, obtain an Employer Identification Number (EIN) from the IRS, which is available at www.irs.gov. The EIN is required for establishing payroll taxation and is required by customers and many vendors.

Any other agreements among the founders (such as roles and responsibilities, compensation, voting requirements, capital commitments, etc.) should be documented in writing and signed by all relevant parties. Verbal agreements made at formation are often remembered differently by different the parties involved. Years in the future these different memories can become a significant source of disagreement and unnecessary litigation if agreements aren't memorialized in writing.

> *Story: An enterprise software company raised angel capital and planned to start selling a revolutionary technology. But the 2 founders had significantly different views on how the company would be run, what the key features of the product needed to be, and how to go to market with marketing, sales and channel. After nine months of internal squabbling among the 2 founders, about which of them were responsible for each of the different aspects of the company's business, the business had failed to make meaningful progress. Thus, having not completed the product nor made any sales, the company ran out of money and closed its doors for good. All because key agreements, roles and responsibilities were not hammered out and agreed upon before getting started.*

Dun & Bradstreet

Dun & Bradstreet (D&B) provides credit monitoring services to companies and individuals. All companies receive a unique D&B number (called a DUNS number). When starting a business, go to www.dnb.com to obtain a DUNS number for your business at no cost. Doing so requires providing certain basic information about the business. D&B offers many paid services to monitor your company's credit, but generally as a startup with poor credit, these services are unnecessary.

At least annually use D&B's iUpdate service to update your D&B credit file at no cost. Be aware that customers, suppliers and competitors have access to this data, so provide no sensitive data that could be used against your business. Rather provide accurate and important information that's not so sensitive.

Other Formation Issues

A company is obligated to establish tax relationships almost immediately upon formation. Income tax returns (Federal and State) will need to be filed starting with the first year in business. Many local jurisdictions (such as City and County) have requirements for establishing local property tax and occupation tax reporting. A company with employees is required to register for payroll tax withholding and reporting. Playbook 7 addresses taxation.

Establish a business bank account for the business separate from your personal bank accounts. Ideally establish separate business credit cards too, or at a minimum document business expenses paid by personal credit card and seek reimbursement from the company's accounting using a simple expense reimbursement form. Failure to maintain the business finances separate from personal finances can cause all sorts of issues with investors and taxing authorities.

Accounting: Secrets your CPA Doesn't Tell You

This chapter on Accounting addresses the following topics:

- Accounting system
- Customer invoicing
- Vendors & payables
- Payroll
- Monthly closing & financial reporting
- Audit, review or compilation

Accounting is like the scoreboard in a sporting event, it keeps track of the money (being made and being spent) so entrepreneurs and investors know how the business is doing. Accounting is also the language of business and so all entrepreneurs must understand at least the basics.

Key accounting tasks to be performed include:

Accounting system

The basic starting point of an accounting function is the accounting system used to track all transactions and report on the company's financial health. Choose a simple, standard, inexpensive accounting package. QuickBooks is the de facto gold standard for small businesses, offering both an online hosted version and traditional on-premise software licenses. QuickBooks offers several versions with different features and capabilities at different price points. Most startup tech companies start with a basic QuickBooks package and subsequently upgrade for added functionality later if needed. More about QuickBooks is available at http://quickbooks.intuit.com/.

Use the accounting system to track all company transactions, posting all sales and expenses for the business. Because the business is separate from the entrepreneur or any one person, personal expenses should be kept separate from company expenses and not recorded in the company accounting system. In other words, keep personal car payments, mortgage payments and vacations out of the company's accounting records.

An accounting system requires a chart of accounts, which is a list of the various revenues, expenses, assets and liabilities that-will be tracked. Charts of account include things like bank accounts, accounts receivable, accounts payable, sales, salaries and rent. Most accounting systems have several standard charts of accounts to choose from, which are fine initially for most businesses. A sample chart of accounts for a startup tech company is at Appendix I.

Likewise, most accounting systems allow for use of departments (referred to as classes in QuickBooks) which is another dimension for understanding the business. Using departments can be helpful to further understand where expenses are incurred. For example, salaries may be a big portion of total expenses, but more specifically salaries for the product development department is a majority of total salary expense. A common departmental structure for technology companies include Sales, Marketing, Product Development, Professional Services, Customer Success and General/Admin.

> *Story: A founder of a software/hardware appliance business was an engineer by training and wanted to save money, so rather than using an accounting system he entered all expenses for his startup into a spreadsheet, believing this was proper accounting. Because of his engineering mindset, the spreadsheet was meticulous and accurate to the penny. But when prospective investors asked basic questions such as how much the company had spent on product development, or what the monthly burn rate was, the entrepreneur and his spreadsheet weren't able to answer the questions posed. So, the company recreated the accounting records in a system that would produce standard accounting analyses and reports.*

Customer invoicing

Once the accounting system has been established, use it to record business activity. Plan to invoice customers regularly, accurately and timely. Every company has a different cycle; some invoice daily, some invoice weekly, some invoice monthly. For a large transaction, invoice the customer immediately upon receipt of an order to improve cash flow. The sooner a customer is invoiced, the sooner the business can collect the funds. Request prompt payment terms and payment of funds via electronic transfer (such as EFT) when possible.

Companies with a large volume of relatively small customer invoices must automate the process of billing customers and posting cash to the customer's account. These types of transactions are often paid by credit cards which are processed automatically by a third-party credit card processor. While this simplifies the actual invoicing and collection, there are costs and risks. Processing via credit cards will cost of 2-3% in processing fees. There's a risk of chargebacks, customers that later deny the charge with their credit card company, and there needs to be a reconciliation between the billing system and cash collected to ensure all sales turn to cash.

Businesses with annual contracts (such as software companies with annual maintenance and support or subscription agreements), invoice customers 30-60 days in advance of the renewal date. Ideally the customer knows about and approves the renewal prior to invoicing.

Where appropriate, retain documentation supporting any numbers or calculations in the customer invoice. For example, professional services businesses that invoice on a time-and-materials basis (i.e. by the hour) typically require timesheets from employees documenting the number of hours of work performed. Having this detail readily accessible will be essential if a customer questions an invoice or has the right to audit timesheets, terms upon which many large customers insist.

Unfortunately, not every customer pays their invoice fully or on time. Payment delays could be caused by dissatisfaction with the solution, a customer's desire to stretch vendors or failure to properly process the invoice. Regular communication with past due customer is essential. Some large customers have a bad habit of paying only the squeaky wheels so timely follow up regarding past due invoices is essential.

Communication with past due customers can begin with a gentle reminder and request of the customer's business people who purchased the solution, to ensure they've approved the invoice for payment with their accounting department. Communicate with the customer's accounting department to check on payment status, whether the invoice is in the system, whether the invoice has been approved for payment and when the invoice is scheduled to be paid. Accounting departments can't pay invoices without approval, but they can share a lot of good information about why an invoice has not been paid. Often one or two friendly reminders is sufficient to get past due invoices paid.

To ensure the team is aware of payment delays, send the Accounts Receivable Aging from the accounting system to management and the sales team regularly, at least monthly. These individuals have relationships with the customer and can help when collections issues arise. While nobody likes making collection calls, everyone in a small company must understand the difference between booking a sale and having the cash to spend for things like payroll. By sharing this detail regularly there should be no surprises later if a customer defaults on payment.

In the accounting system, regularly post cash receipts to the customer's account so the list of outstanding invoices is up to date. Regularly and promptly deposit funds received into the bank. A trusted party other than the bookkeeper (such as the entrepreneur) should handle all cash receipts and make the bank deposit, to segregate responsibilities. These steps keep cash flowing into the business, reduces the risk of funds being misappropriated and ensure records are accurate and timely.

Many businesses are obligated to invoice and collect state and local sales taxes. See Playbook 7 for further discussion of sales taxes.

Vendors & payables

Regularly enter vendor invoices and employee expense reimbursement requests into accounting system as accounts payable. For any new vendor, request a completed and signed Form W-9 before paying any money to the vendor. The completed Form W-9 is essential since the IRS requires reporting of payments made to vendors on Form 1099-MISC subsequent to year-end. The IRS Form W-9 is available at www.irs.gov.

Vendor invoices should be dated in the accounting system using the invoice date or the date services were rendered so the expense appears in the proper accounting period. A manager in the business (for a small company the CEO or VP level personnel) approves each invoice prior to payment, ensuring the expense is valid and that goods or services have been received. A manager's approval ensures that only valid vendor invoices are paid and minimizes the risk of cash being paid to an unauthorized party.

Vendor invoices should be paid regularly, often in a weekly check run covering only invoices that have been approved and are due. Invoices that have not reached their due date or have not been approved by a manager should not be paid. Whether payment is made by check, online bill pay, wire transfer or ACH, there should be a very limited set of authorized signatories. For small companies, the CEO is typically the primary signatory as an internal control feature.

Payroll

Companies must regularly and routinely pay their employees. To comply with labor laws, paying employees requires a set of complex calculations around tax withholdings (federal, state and local), medical benefits, 401K, etc. Most companies outsource payroll processing (including payment of net compensation, filing of payroll tax returns, etc.) to a third-party firm such as ADP or Paychex since the process of complying with tax obligations (withholding, remitting and reporting) is so complex across all 50 U.S. States in addition to local (city and county) jurisdictions.

Newer online-oriented payroll providers such as BambooHR, Zenefits and Gusto have been formed lately to simplify payroll processing for small businesses. Many offer modern, online architecture and will integrate not just payroll processing, but also other Human Resources functions such as employee onboarding and termination, employee benefits, dashboards, etc.

> *Story: A training software company sold its assets to a large and well-capitalized competitor as part of a roll-up strategy. Several years later the training software company's accountants received a payroll deficiency letter from the State Department of Revenue claiming the company had failed to pay a few hundred dollars of payroll taxes several years in the past, before the company's assets were sold. Because the accountants had copies of the payroll tax filings which were filed by the third party payroll provider, they were able to address the deficiency. Without copies of the payroll reports, the former directors and officers of the company may have been personally liable for payroll tax deficiencies.*

Often employee expense reimbursements and incentive compensation (bonuses and commissions) are paid through payroll rather than accounts payable to streamline the disbursement and reporting process. This requires expense reports or incentive calculations be submitted and approved several days prior to processing of payroll.

Certain paperwork is required of employees at the time of hire. See Playbook 4 for further discussion of employment paperwork requirements.

Monthly closing & financial reporting

The accounting books are closed monthly to ensure an accurate balance sheet and P&L each month. A simple checklist should be established and used each month to ensure a complete and accurate closing. The monthly closing process typically includes the following:

- Reconcile all bank and credit card accounts.
- Review the accounts receivable aging for accuracy, an understanding of which customers owe money and whether any collectability issues exist.
- Substantiate all balance sheet accounts with supporting documentation such as statements and/or spreadsheets.
- Review income statement accounts compared to budget to ensure appropriateness of each expense in proper accounts. Review the income statement accounts compared to the previous month to ensure appropriateness of each expense in proper accounts.
- Especially tricky accounts should be reviewed in further detail. For most high-tech companies, revenue recognition

is a complex accounting issue that must be addressed and substantiated each month.

- If the accounting system allows periods to be locked down and uneditable, do it. Locking down previous monthly helps to ensure past period numbers don't accidentally change over time.

A sample closing checklist is at <u>Appendix II</u>.

Once the books are closed for a month, distribute a standard monthly financial package to the executive team including key reports such as:

Monthly financial package:

From the accounting system:

- Income statement: for the month, quarter and year to date compared to budget
- Balance sheet: for the month compared to budget
- Statement of cash flows: for the month, quarter and year to date compared to budget

From outside of the accounting system:

- Headcount by department: compared to budget
- Highlights: a plain English bullet point summary of key points that occurred in the business during the period. Use this to explain any significant variances

from budget or any large one-time items affecting the numbers.

- Key performance metrics (a/k/a key performance indicators or KPI's): every business has numerous key performance metrics that are often outside of finance and accounting and should be tracked and reported. An example of key performance metrics for a tech company is at Appendix III.

All financial reporting for management and accounting purposes should be accrual-basis. Cash-basis financial reporting may be acceptable for tax purposes (see Playbook 7 for further discussion regarding taxes). Investors and acquirers will insist on accrual-basis financial statements.

The reports from the accounting system can all be set up as "push button" reporting and generated quite simple as standard reports out of the system. The other reports external to the accounting system should be quick and easy to develop and populate with updated data monthly.

The books should be closed, and reports distributed promptly after the end of each calendar month, typically in about 15-20 days or less. The quicker the books are closed, the more valuable the information to management for decision-making. Key management should review the reports together to understand the business financial status, including cash position and significant deviations from expectations.

Audit, review or compilation

An audit is a detailed examination of the company's financial statements by an independent public accounting firm, with the goal of the accounting firm expressing an opinion on the fairness of the financial reporting.

An accountant's review is a less-detailed examination of the company's financial statements by an independent public accounting firm, with the goal of the accounting firm expressing not an opinion on the fairness of the financial reporting, but rather a statement that the firm isn't aware of any issues in the financial statements.

A compilation is simply an accounting firm's issuance of the company's financial statements in proper accounting format, with no expression of opinion or fairness.

Any company following basic accounting procedures as set forth in this text would not need to pay an accounting firm to do a compilation. Audits and/or reviews are always good internal procedures for ensuring the financial statements are presented appropriately, but most small companies and start-ups don't spend the money for an audit or review. Once sophisticated third party investors are involved, then typically an annual audit is required.

Corporate Finance: Ensuring that Cash is King

This chapter on Corporate Finance addresses the following topics:

- Budget & financial plan
- Corporate insurance
- 13-week cash forecast
- Treasury

Whereas the purpose of accounting is to record and report transactions that occur in the business, the purpose of corporate finance is to manage the company's cash and project business results going forward for planning reasons.

Key corporate finance tasks to be performed include:

Budget & financial plan

Every business needs a budget (a.k.a. a financial plan). The budget sets expectations for the year about various topics such as revenues, expenses necessary to achieve that revenue target and cash needs for the year. Using spreadsheets, a simple monthly budget can be developed. Ideally this first means setting business goals and objectives for the period, which are part of the vision for the next year. The budget is a financial representation of what is required to achieve those goals, and what the financial results will look like. The budget provides visibility into the year's finances and becomes a tool against which progress towards goals is measured.

A budget should be developed with input from the management team, ultimately with the CEO having final authority to make decisions regarding allocation of limited capital towards varying internal goals.

It's common that Sales leadership wants to hire more Sales personnel; Marketing leadership wants to invest significant money in new marketing and advertising to drive leader; Product leadership wants to hire more software engineers, etc. If all executives from all departments got their entire "wish list" of investment opportunities, most small tech companies would quickly be out of cash and out of business. This is where the CEO must become the final arbiter of deciding where to allocate precious capital, and which initiatives to fund now or delay until later or cut entirely.

Often a budget is established at the beginning of a year for the current calendar year. Even better, the budget can be updated each quarter to maintain a rolling 4 quarter forecast so there's always visibility into the next 12 months' finances. When raising capital from outside investors, a financial plan may be as lengthy as 5 years although accuracy will decrease dramatically beyond the next 12-18 months. And for a very early stage start-up a budget is complete guesswork without any history on which to base assumptions.

In budgeting, use the same chart of accounts and department structure as in the accounting system so reporting results compared to budget becomes much simpler. The budget should include several printable spreadsheets such as:

- Projected financial statements including P&L, balance sheet and statement of cash flows by month, quarter and full year. While common for start-ups, a budget without a balance sheet or cash flows is an incomplete picture of the company's finances and fails to forecast the company's most important asset, its cash.
- Summarize key performance metrics by month, quarter and the full year as appropriate. See <u>Appendix III</u> for sample key performance metrics.
- Summarize major assumptions such as number of new customers, average selling price, headcount by department, etc.

Once finished, a budget is presented to the Board of Directors for approval, then entered into the accounting system for comparative financial reporting. The smaller the company and the simpler that operations are, the simpler the budget spreadsheets can be. Once outside investors are involved, typically there's more scrutiny into the planning process, key assumptions and major risks.

Story: An early-stage business intelligence software company sought growth capital from a private equity (PE) firm. The PE firm falsely assumed that the company was unsophisticated, and its financial projections included an income statement but no cash flow nor balance sheet. Upon questioning from the PE firm, the company indicated that their financial model included all these elements. The PE firm were skeptical and in disbelief. After reviewing the model, they were impressed with the company's financial management and continued their pursuit of the company.

Corporate insurance

Every company needs insurance to meet statutory and contractual requirements and to manage risks in the business. An insurance broker who specializes in company (not personal) insurance can secure the necessary coverage.

Essential insurance coverages include:

- Workers compensation coverage is mandated by law and protects employees that are injured at work
- Business package policy includes general liability and property insurance is mandated by most customers and landlords.

Optional insurance coverages include:

- Errors & omissions (E&O a.k.a. professional liability) protects against damage caused by the company's product or negligence of professionals in providing services. Corporate customers may mandate this type of coverage which regardless is wise to implement once there's significant revenue streams.

- Directors & officers (D&O) insurance with employment practices liability (EPL) protects directors and officers from claims based on securities litigation and employment-related harassment, two of the more common types of claims against directors and officers personally. Outside Board members may mandate this type of coverage, which regardless is wise once the company's headcount increases significantly and/or there are major external investors.

- Key person life insurance provides a sum of money should a named key executive pass away. The purpose of key person life is to provide funds for the company to locate a suitable replacement and sustain itself during the period of transition without such key person.

As a company goes global (see Playbook 9) ensure your customers, employees and property are adequately insured beyond the United States by discussing with your insurance team.

13-week cash forecast

Cash is the life blood of any company; without cash a company can't pay employees, buy supplies, pay rent or literally keep the lights on. When cash is tight, prepare a 13-week cash forecast and update it weekly. The cash forecast provides visibility into the company's cash position for the next 3 months. Without visibility, an executive is flying blind and without key information for deciding whether to hire or fire employees, whether to expand or shrink or how much money is needed to keep the business afloat.

The 13-week cash forecast can and should be simple, and rolls forward the cash balance each week, as follows:

- The beginning of the week's cash balance
- Add expected cash receipts from outstanding customer invoices
- Add expected cash receipts from existing customer renewals
- Add expected cash receipts from new sales
- Subtract expected cash disbursements
- Equals the ending cash balance for that week.

Some facts are known about weekly cash flow, others must be assumed. Typically, expenses are more predictable since payroll and other monthly expenses usually don't vary much from month to month. With some payment history or standard payment terms, collection of existing accounts receivable can be estimated with a degree of accuracy. Collection of new sales activity is much harder to forecast and predict since that requires forecasting both the new sales booking and also the subsequent collection.

When cash is tight, and a CEO is concerned about the ability to meet payroll obligations, look at the cash forecast from a very conservative perspective. This may mean including no new sales in the cash forecast. A cash forecast that shows an ending cash balance greater than zero each week indicates that the company will survive at least in the short term.

A cash forecast that shows an ending cash balance less than zero in any week indicates the amount of cash the business needs to survive. The needed cash may come from reduced costs, increased new sales, faster customer collections, delayed disbursements or new capital. A forecasted negative cash balance gives management a target for which to strive. Most small tech companies are undercapitalized and thus always nearly out of cash.

A simple 13-week cash forecast in place can be easily modified to run several scenarios to understand the sensitivity towards collections, disbursements, etc.

Story: A technology services company was profitable and growing rapidly. Their monthly financial analysis included an income statement and balance sheet, but no projection of future cash position. After finishing a tremendous growth year with record profits, the company needed to pay out significant bonuses in the following January because of the record growth. These bonuses caused the company to spend nearly all of its available cash and the company could barely meet its monthly payroll obligations. Had the company been forecasting cash it would have been aware of the cash shortfall months beforehand, to seek alternatives.

Treasury

The treasury function in a business moves money around across different banks and geographies as needed. Most small tech companies are small enough that the treasury function is simple and straightforward.

Any excess cash can be invested in a save online savings account that (i) spreads the risk of bank default across multiple institutions and (ii) earns interest income (although typically very little). Rarely will small tech companies have sufficient cash and visibility to long term financial plans to lock their cash in CD's or other fixed instruments that limit access to the cash.

A minimum level of cash will be required in each bank and in each country in which the company operates and some countries have a minimal capital requirement to even maintain the business itself.

Human Resources: Best Practices to Hire & Fire Without Getting Sued

This chapter on Human Resources addresses the following topics:

- Offer letter
- Employee handbook
- Covenants agreement
- Medical benefits
- Employment termination
- Exempt vs non-exempt
- Organization chart

In high tech businesses, a company's most valuable assets are its people who create the products and service customers.

Key human resources tasks to be performed include:

Offer letter

To hire an employee, present the candidate with an offer letter that complies with state and federal regulations. The offer letter summarizes the basics about job such as:

- the employee's name and contact information
- the company's name and contract information
- the role and title for which the employee is being hired
- a summary of job responsibilities
- a summary of compensation and benefits
- expected start date
- expected number of hours per week (for hourly non-exempt employees)
- "at-will" status
- signatures
- expiration date for acceptance of the offer

In most jurisdictions in the U.S., the offer letter includes the term "at-will" indicating that the employment relationship can be terminated by either party at any time, that there's no long term contractual commitment to the employment. An offer letter form document can be created for standard company terms and modified slightly for each new hire.

A sample offer letter for an exempt U.S. at-will employee is at Appendix IV.

Hourly non-exempt offer letters should include language that no overtime is expected or authorized without express written approval from the candidate's supervisor.

Employee handbook

Companies create an employee handbook to summarize key company policies and procedures, and to document the company's position on important employment-related regulatory matters. The handbook includes provisions on legal issues such as equal employment, harassment and discrimination, as well as provisions on employment such as holiday and vacation pay, work hours and smoking regulations.

The handbook can be simple and good example of employee handbooks are available from the Society for Human Resource Management (SHRM) at www.shrm.org and from Entrepreneur Magazine at www.entrepreneur.com among other places. The handbook should be distributed to all employees and updated as needed. Employees must acknowledge receipt of the handbook and agree to comply with its terms. Major revisions to the handbook should be acknowledged by employees as well.

Initially company may skip the action of creating an employee handbook until it has hired a sufficient number of employees to justify the time and cost.

a) Compliance paperwork

Certain paperwork is required by law for each employee, such as:

- Completed Form I-9 validating the employee's right to work in the U.S.A. The form and detailed instructions are available from U.S. Citizenship and Immigration Services division of the Department of Homeland Security at www.uscis.gov. Certain companies, including those with at least 50 employees, are required to validate the right to work in the U.S.A. using an online system called eVerify (see www. everify.gov).

- Completed Form W-4 documenting the employee's number of dependents for federal tax purposes (which affects payroll withholdings). The form and instructions are available from the IRS website at www.irs.gov.
- Completed state withholding form documenting the employee's number of dependents for state tax purposes (which affects payroll withholdings). These state forms are usually available from the state's department of revenue website.
- Completed Form W-9 for non-employee contractors providing a tax identification number (which is necessary to issue Form 1099-MISC, see Playbook 7 for discussion regarding tax compliance). The form and instructions are available from the IRS website at www.irs.gov.

Covenants agreements

In tech companies, employees sign employment covenants paperwork (known as restrictive covenants) at the time of accepting the job offer. The covenants paperwork is not required by statute but is a best practice that ensures:

- Employee's assignment of intellectual property to the company (rather than the employee owning the results of his or her work product)
- Nondisclosure of confidential information

- Nonsolicitation of employees and customers to reduce the likelihood of an employee competing with the company for customers or employees
- Noncompetition is sometimes included as a further means of restricting the employee but is especially tricky in many states based on local laws

Each non-employee independent contractor should sign covenants paperwork at the time of agreeing to work with company which includes the same types of restrictions required of employees.

> *Story: A data quality software company hired a new sales executive but failed to realize that the new employee didn't sign the employment covenants paperwork upon being hired. Years later, as part of an HR audit in preparation for being acquired, the missing employment covenants agreement was noticed. The employee refused to sign the agreement at that stage, eventually bringing in his own lawyer to negotiate with company counsel. Eventually, after many months of distraction, effort and legal cost, the employee tried to blackmail the company before seeking employment with a competitor.*

Medical benefits

Most but not all companies offer some medical benefits to employees, especially in companies that seek highly-educated, highly-skilled employees who could work elsewhere. A benefits broker who works with small businesses (ideally in the industry) can help locate appropriate medical coverage.

The Affordable Care Act and its repeal has made medical benefits more complicated to manage and costs for medical coverage continue to rise. But benefits are essential to attracting and retaining high-quality employees.

The first step with medical benefits is to decide on what coverage to offer. Consider medical, dental, vision, 401K, flex spending, short term disability, long term disability, life insurance, etc. Decide what portion the company will pay and what portion the employee will pay for coverage each month. Often small high-tech companies pay a high portion (75-100%) of the employee's coverage but a smaller portion (0-50%) of coverage for dependents. As the number of employees in the business grows, consider offering multiple plans, one being a basic plan that the company pays for, and a second plan being more comprehensive that employees can choose to pay more for.

Your benefits broker (as well as newly hired employees) can be a great source of market intelligence about what other companies offer in terms of employee benefits. Think about what companies you compete with for employee talent, and ensure your benefits program is at least competitive.

Typically, medical benefits are only available to full-time employees of the company, which means those working at least 30 hours a week for the company. Independent contractors and part-time employees who work less than 30 hours a week are not eligible for medical benefits. If a company has a medical benefits plan, typically it must be offered to all full-time employees.

Employment termination

Unfortunately, sometimes a person's job performance doesn't meet expectations and the employment relationship must be terminated. Termination of employment must be for legitimate business reasons and never for discriminatory reasons. Being terminated can be a major stress event for an employee and occasionally an employee will react with significant negative emotion upon termination.

Regular formal and informal feedback between a supervisor and employee are essential and a best practice for all managers. These discussions should help to clarify an employee's role and expectations and validate how the employee is performing relative to those expectations.

Prior to concluding that employment termination is appropriate, discuss verbally and document in writing with the employee what expectations for that role are being achieved and which are not being achieved. This is called a performance improvement plan and ideally should be signed by the employee. Give the employee a reasonable period to improve performance to meet the standards and expectations for that role in the company. Offer to help the employee achieve the desired level of performance but remember that the burden to perform to expectations is on employee, not the manager.

If employment is terminated, offer separation pay (often 2 weeks of base salary) in exchange for a signed, written waiver and release. The written waiver and release is a complex legal document by which the employee waives the right to sue the company for employment-related claims such as discrimination or harassment. Legal involvement is essential to ensure enforceability in Federal and State courts.

Provide written notice to the employee regarding termination including the date of termination, status of medical and other benefits, etc. Remind the employee about confidentiality and nonsolicitation obligations as well.

When an employee leaves the company for any reason (voluntary or not), communicate the employee's departure promptly to key stakeholders and other employees. The departed employee's responsibilities need to be divvied up and consideration given when to hire a replacement.

Exempt vs. non-exempt

While most executives consider employees either salaried or hourly, the Federal Department of Labor designates employees in different categories, either exempt or non-exempt.

Non-exempt employees are required to receive overtime pay for hours worked beyond a normal work week. Overtime pay is a requirement for these employees regardless of whether the employee is considered an hourly employee or salaried. On the other hand, employers are not obligated to pay overtime to exempt employees for hours worked beyond a normal work week.

Generally exempt employees include executives, professionals, computer employees, highly compensated employees, outside sales employees and the like, whereas non-exempt employees include everyone else. The Federal laws regarding overtime are complex and more information can be found at the U.S. Department of Labor at www.dol.gov.

Many early-stage technology companies with largely a highly-educated, highly-paid workforce will classify every employee as exempt. While that strategy is not in strict conformance with federal or state laws, the practice is common.

Organization chart

A company should maintain and continually update an organization chart, showing key management roles and reporting responsibilities. An example of an organization chart is below:

Sample organization chart.

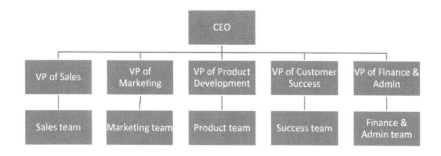

Investors will be interested in the org chart for executive management roles and will be keen to understand who the key employees are.

Likewise, each employee should understand very clearly to whom he or she reports to maximize communication and clarity.

Legal: Avoid Risk Without Breaking the Bank

This chapter on Legal addresses the following topics:

- Customer agreements
- Employment-related agreements
- Vendor agreements
- Capital raises
- Intellectual property

Business arrangements with customers, suppliers and employees are usually documented in written contractual agreements.

Key legal tasks to be performed include:

Customer agreements

It's imperative that any business have clear contractual terms and conditions with customers. An attorney experienced in the company's field can draft form customer agreements for use with customers. Typically for software companies form customer agreements include the following:

- Software license or subscription agreement
- Consulting services agreement
- Nondisclosure agreement

These agreements are incorporated into terms of service for companies that operate primarily via the internet, such as most SaaS companies. Having standard agreements with a "click-wrap" upon download or terms of service for an internet site can mitigate the need to negotiate contractual terms individually with each customer.

Ownership of intellectual property is a key concern for all companies, especially technology companies that rely on intellectual property as their primary asset. Where possible limit warranties, damages and remedies, and try to mandate use of local jurisdiction and local law in the event of a dispute.

When working with large corporate customers, contractual terms are laboriously negotiated and agreed up, but once signed rarely looked at again. The larger the customer and larger the dollar volume of purchases, the more likely a customer will negotiate standard terms (or require compliance with their standard terms).

Many big companies have a big procurement and contracting process which is designed to slow down transactions and extract the best possible deal for the customer. Avoiding these processes if all possible is wise. Using click-wrap agreement and/or online terms of service can sometimes bypass the slow, bureaucratic procurement process and speed the path to closing sales deals.

Story: An insurance software company believed in the Do-It-Yourself model of legal contracts, having created its own sale contract from one sourced on the internet. But the founder didn't realize that a sale contract means selling software rather than licensing it, and that customers may thus actually have owned the software's source code. When discovered by investors in due diligence, the investors quickly backed away from the company and declined to invest.

Employment-related agreements

Likewise, it's imperative that any business have clear terms of employment with all employees. An attorney experienced in the company's field can draft form employment-related agreements for use with employees. For high tech businesses form employment agreements often include the following:

- Offer letter
- Employment covenants
- Contractor agreements
- Employee handbook
- Stock option plan and form stock option grant agreements

Ownership of intellectual property is a key for all companies, especially technology companies that rely on intellectual property as their primary asset. These documents can ensure that employment is "at-will" whenever possible. See Playbook 4 for more discussion regarding employment-related agreements.

Vendor agreements

Likewise, it's imperative that any business have clear terms of agreement with key vendors and suppliers. Frequently vendors will provide their form agreement which is one-sided rather than fair and balanced. For large purchases and purchases of key components, negotiate the vendor's form agreement and use an attorney if necessary to understand complex legal matters. Always read the fine print and ensure that ownership of intellectual property is clear and addressed in writing.

Sometimes vendor terms are non-negotiable, other times the terms are negotiable. If the stated boilerplate terms are not acceptable, it never hurts to try to negotiate. Often a vendor's sales team will state that terms are boilerplate, making you think they are non-negotiable. This is nearly always to their benefit, not yours, and may be more negotiable than the sales person wants you to think.

Capital raises

Raising capital – both debt and equity – requires use of attorneys experienced with the complex state and federal securities laws. Every capital raise, no matter who the investor is or what the size of the offering is, must comply with existing statutes. Most capital raises can be completed with little added cost or time by lawyers. Violating securities laws can pose big headaches with regulators, investors (especially if the investment should ever sour) or future acquirers.

Don't make the common mistake of assuming that a small capital raise from a friend or family member can be done without involvement from a lawyer. Working with the right lawyer is a key, one who understands the securities laws and a small business mentality of needing to keep costs low.

The securities laws a very complex and legal advice on how to raise capital can be intimidating and sound expensive. But an experienced securities lawyer can simply the issues and document the transaction to keep you and your investor out of trouble.

> *Story: A prospective investor in a blockchain company claimed he didn't need to comply with securities laws because of the nature of the transaction being more than just a capital raise, and thus refused to sign the proposed investment contract paperwork. Company counsel, who was trained in securities laws, found a workaround that was acceptable to the investor, so the company could pursue the capital raise while having ensured compliance with all applicable laws.*

Intellectual property

Intellectual property can include patents, trademarks, copyrights and the like. Registering intellectual property for protection under state or federal laws requires experienced intellectual property attorneys. Patent filings can get very expensive so determine an intellectual property strategy before engaging too deeply on seeking protection.

Most companies have intellectual property. Choosing whether to pursue protection for these assets is an economic one for each business, based on the expected cost of pursuing protection compared to the expected value in the future of such protection.

Governance: Build a Foundation for Corporate Professionalism

This chapter on Governance addresses the following topics:

- Board & Shareholder meetings
- Minutes
- Corporate minute book

Corporate governance includes actions of the company's shareholders and board of directors which govern the company's overall structure and direction.

Key governance tasks to be performed include:

Board and Shareholder meetings

Typically, companies hold meetings of the board of directors (called board of managers for LLC's) at least annually. Outside investors often require board meetings more frequently, perhaps as often as monthly, to monitor the company's progress towards business goals. Members of the board of directors are appointed by shareholder vote.

Meetings of shareholders are less frequent and usually held on an as-needed basis. With outside investors who hold seats on the board of directors, board and shareholder meetings can look very similar.

Properly prepare for board and shareholder meetings, especially if attendees are not involved in the company day-to-day. Send written materials to all attendees at least 48-72 hours in advance of meeting. Confirm the date, time and location of the meeting with each participant including a telephone dial-in number or webinar information if any participants will be remote.

Sending materials ahead of time allows attendees to review and digest the materials beforehand and focus the meeting on productive discussions rather than simply stating facts about recent performance.

For regular meetings, these written materials send ahead of time may include:

- Letter from CEO presenting an update on the business and a summary of key topics to be discussed
- Proposed agenda and timeline for the meeting
- Updated financial statements and key performance indicators
- List of items proposed for discussion and approval

Focus meetings on a discussion of company strategy, resolution of outstanding strategic issues and how board members can help the company, rather than just updating participants on what's new since the last meeting. Don't let meetings become a grade school report on "what I did on my summer vacation."

Sharp and experience operationally-oriented Board members often want to drive Board discussion into tactical and operational details with which they are familiar and experienced. Ideally present this information to Board members in advance of the meeting and address questions before they arise. Then your time with the Board can be focused on more strategic topics.

Board meetings should have no surprises. Bad news must be communicated to board members promptly and ahead of time.

Outside of the formal board and shareholder meetings, communicate with these key individuals informally by phone and email regularly. Solicit input and feedback where someone can help. Ensure the board and key shareholders are up to speed on the status of the company's cash position, especially if cash is tight or the financial future uncertain.

Some board members may become a sounding board or mentor to the CEO. While not a required governance function, this mentoring can be a huge value to the CEO, both from learning from on-the-job performance and getting further insight into how a board member or investor thinks about various situations.

Minutes

Meeting minutes are written in a formal style then submitted for approval at a subsequent meeting. Usually minutes document little of the detailed discussion during a meeting, but instead summarize generally the topics discussed, and document any resolutions reached. Resolutions typically require the vote of a majority attendees with a quorum in attendance.

In drafting minutes, the company Secretary should keep in mind that minutes may be subpoenaed in the event of significant litigation or claims against the company or its directors and officers. Thus, minutes should be properly prepared for each meeting.

Most jurisdictions allow for board resolutions in form of a unanimous written consent in lieu of a Board meeting. So, it's possible to solicit a board vote without a formal meeting but doing so requires written approval by all board members, rather than just a majority.

Similarly, most jurisdictions allow for shareholder resolutions in the form of majority written consent in lieu of a shareholder meeting. Non-consenting shareholders must be provided written notice of the actions taken without their consent.

File all minutes and written consents of the board and shareholders in the corporate minute book.

> Story: A digital media software company was very
> informal in its governance style. Board meetings were
> rarely held, and when they did occur, documentation
> of the meeting was light and focused on business
> matters without proper governance procedures.
> As a results employee stock option grants were
> never formally approved by the Board. Rather the
> Board were notified of stock options informally, but

never asked for approvals. During due diligence, a prospective buyer concluded that employee stock options were never approved as required and thus could not be exercised for a profit by employees. Despite strenuous objections from the company, the buyer would not relent, and the company had to find a workaround for employees to profit financially from the acquisition.

Corporate minute book

The corporate minute book is a register of all corporate governance materials for the company starting with inception. The corporate minute book includes items such as:

- Bylaws and amendments
- Articles of incorporation and amendments (or operating agreement for LLC's)
- Board minutes and consents
- Shareholder minutes and consents
- Securities (debt and equity) offering documents
- Stock option plan and grants
- Merger & acquisition agreements
- Debt agreements
- Copies of stock certificates issued

Taxes & Licenses: What's Required and What Can Wait

This chapter on Taxes & Licenses addresses the following topics:

- Year-end federal income tax returns
- Year-end State income tax returns
- Annual State business license
- Sales taxes
- Payroll taxes
- Contractors and vendors

All businesses in the U.S.A. are required to comply with a complex set of federal, state and local tax and licensing obligations.

Key tax and licensing tasks to be performed include:

Year-end federal income tax returns

For businesses, Federal income tax returns are due by April 15 of the following year (for calendar year businesses). Many businesses file for and receive a 6-month extension to delay the date by which returns must be filed. Profitable companies may owe up to 35%

of net taxable income to the IRS, plus additional state and local taxes. The federal marginal tax rates for businesses are among the highest in the world, but the U.S. tax system is very complex and allows for a significant number of deductions to reduce net taxable income.

The Tax Cuts and Jobs Act implemented in January 2018 reduced tax rates for some companies, but also added complexity for U.S. tax filers. Federal and State tax laws are constantly evolving and changing, and the provisions in this tax may be out of date by the time they are consumed.

For unprofitable companies, no Federal taxes are usually owed but returns still must be filed. For these early-stage unprofitable high-tech companies, the biggest federal tax issues are often:

- Research & experimentation (R&E) tax credits: Companies can receive federal tax credits for performing research and experimentation activities. For an unprofitable company, these credits can be useful and financially worthwhile after the company turns profitable.
- Utilization of Net Operating Loss upon a change of control: Unprofitable companies generate Net Operating Losses, which are the accumulation of net losses over time. Upon a chance of control in the company, the ability to use these Net Operating Losses is limited.
- Change from cash to accrual method of accounting for tax purposes: Start-up companies often file tax returns on a cash-basis but are permitted once to switch to

accrual-basis reporting. A company will make the switch when advantageous.

- Deferral of start-up expenses: Certain expenses are not tax deductible until the company has started operations. These costs are deferred for tax purposes rather than being expensed as incurred.

Profitable businesses must remit a quarterly estimate of taxes owed each quarter of the fiscal year.

Companies typically outsource Federal income tax compliance to a trusted and qualified CPA firm.

Year-end State income tax returns

State income tax returns are due at the same time that Federal income tax returns are due. State income tax returns are typically filed in states where the company is operating and has employees.

Profitable companies may owe 3-6% or more of net taxable income to the various states. A company operating in multiple states will apportion (allocate) revenue and profits among the states to determine which states are owed taxes.

Many states impose a minimum level of taxes owed (hundreds or a few thousand dollars) even for unprofitable companies.

Profitable businesses remit a quarterly estimate of taxes owed each quarter of the fiscal year.

Companies typically outsource State income tax compliance to a trusted and qualified CPA firm.

Annual State business license

Companies must register to do business in each state where the company is doing business. Hiring the first employee in a state is the usual trigger for registering to do business in the state, since at that time the business is required to register for payroll and sales taxes there as well. A third-party company known as a registered agent will act on a company's behalf in states where the office location is simply someone's home office. It's important to have a physical mailing address in each State and to be sure that a responsible corporate executive or officer receives all important mailings. The registered agent performs this role, accepting mail or service (of a lawsuit for example) in the states where the company does business.

Each state requires an annual business license which his typically must be paid in the March to May timeframe each year and requires a small fee. In most states, the local Secretary of State governs registration and annual licenses. Visit the website of the Secretary of State for more information.

Sales taxes

Collection of sales taxes is generally required when a business sells tangible personal property to a customer in a state where the seller has a presence (called "nexus"). Nexus is a term relating to the level of involvement a company has in the state. In short, if a company is registered to do business in a state or spends significant time in the state making sales calls, servicing customers, etc. then it likely has nexus for sales tax purposes.

Sales tax generally applies to the sale of tangible personal property only. Sales tax laws are very complicated and vary not only by state, but also by city and county in some cases, as well as special targeted areas within a region. In total there may be 10,000 or more various jurisdictions with slightly different rules on sales taxes. Needless to say, sales taxes are a very complex topic. Thus, the topic of sales taxes is a major tax diligence item in any M&A transaction.

Tangible personal property includes shipping a CD or providing another tangible medium to a customer. Providing services is not considered tangible personal property and thus not subject to sales taxes in most (but not all) jurisdictions. Electronic download of software and online software subscriptions (i.e. Software-as-a-Service) are a mixed bag depending on the jurisdiction – some consider electronic download of software to be subject to sales tax and some do not. Similarly, for software subscriptions or hosted software, some consider electronic download of software to be subject to sales tax and some do not.

At a minimum, register for sales taxes in the states where the business is registered to do business (i.e. where the business has employees). Then invoice and collect sales tax as appropriate from each customer in those states. Doing so has some administrative cost (taking the time to add tax to each invoice, completing a sales tax return and remitting funds to the government each month, etc.) Alternatively, get a valid exemption certificate from the customer to avoid the need to collect sales taxes from that customer. Exemption certificates are available for things such as resale or certain customers.

Sales tax returns then must be filed, and funds remitted to the appropriate governmental entity, often monthly. Companies that are required to collect, remit and report on sales taxes in a significant number of jurisdictions will often outsource sales tax compliance to a specialized third-party accounting service.

> *Story: A business intelligence software company had not properly addressed sales taxes, assuming incorrectly that a relatively small and unprofitable company selling software would be exempt. During due diligence as part of an acquisition, the buyer recognized the risk of the company's non-compliance and demanded a 7-figure reduction in purchase price to compete for the buyer's additional risk. The seller was eventually able to mitigate the risks and reduce the purchase price reduction by about 80%, but not before a lot of added stress and financial risk.*

Payroll taxes

Payroll tax returns are required for each State and the Federal government either monthly or quarterly. Most companies outsource payroll processing which includes calculation of withholdings, remittance of payroll taxes, filing of payroll tax returns and direct deposit of net compensation of employees. The outsourced payroll processor will generate a year-end Form W-2 for each employee summarizing compensation form the previous year. The Form W-2 must be mailed to each employee by January 31 of each year and details sent to the IRS as well.

Contractors and vendors

Before paying an independent contractor or vendor any money, obtain a completed and signed Form W-9 showing the vendor's tax identification number. By January 31 of each year, a Form 1099-MISC must be prepared and mailed to each contractor summarizing compensation paid in the prior year. By February 28 of each year, a mail Form 1096 summarizing all Forms 1099-MISC must be mailed to the IRS along with a copy of each of the Forms 1099-MISC. Most accounting packages will help prepare the Forms 1099-MISC for vendors paid.

Administration: Keeping It Simple & Effective

This chapter on Administration addresses the following topics:

- Filing systems
- Paper files
- Electronic files

Some simple, regular administrative actions will keep the company's files in good shape when needed for due diligence or audit.

Key administrative tasks to be performed include:

Filing systems

Maintain an orderly scheme for filing and organizing all important corporate paperwork. A typical organization scheme looks like the following:

- Nondisclosure agreements: Maintain a file for all nondisclosure (a.k.a. confidentiality or NDA) agreements signed with customers, vendors, employees, prospects, etc. Organize the files alphabetically by name. An organized system with fully-executed documents will show a third party the seriousness the business takes to maintain confidentiality of proprietary information.

- Customers: Maintain a file for each customer which includes all customer contracts, PO's, SOW's, etc. Organize the files by customer name and then by contract, project or job. Include Statements of Work and all Change Requests (there may be many) if services are involved.

- Vendors: Maintain a file for each vendor or supplier which includes all vendor contracts, including license agreements, leases, service agreements, tax and compliance paperwork (Federal Form W-9), etc. Organize the files by vendor name.

- Employees: Maintain an employee file for each employee which includes signed offer letter, employment covenants paperwork, commissions and/or incentive compensation plans (if any), resignation and/or separation paperwork (if any), stock options grant paperwork (if any), separate arrangements (if any), employee handbook acknowledgement, tax and compliance paperwork (Federal Form I-9, W-4, Georgia G-4). Organize the files by employee last name. Performance-related files for employees are often kept in a separate filing mechanism.

- Independent contractors: Maintain a vendor file for each independent contractor which includes signed contractor or consulting agreement, contractor covenants agreement (assigning intellectual property to the company if applicable), statements of work and tax compliance paperwork (Form W-9). Organize the files by contractor last name.

- Governance: Include all governance paperwork such as bylaws, articles of incorporation, stock option plans, etc. (See Section 5 for corporate record book). Organize the files by type first, then by date.

Paper files

All important paperwork should be kept in hard copy once executed by all parties to the appropriate agreement. While many companies today sign documents electronically and originals don't exist, it can be helpful to have hard copies and not just electronic files. These files should be in a locked cabinet with access limited to only a few people.

Electronic files

An electronic PDF copy of each fully-executed agreement should be stored on company servers in addition to being filed in paper form. Use the same filing structure as the paper filing system and ensure everything is backed up electronically on a regular basis. Limit access to the server which contains this paperwork with password protection.

Story: A small software analytics company did well to keep copies of all contracts with customers and suppliers as well as non-disclosure agreements and employment related paperwork. However not all documents were signed by the company, some only signed by the customer or vendor or employee. And some were in hard copy, some were in PDF/ electronic copy, and some in both. So, during due diligence by a Fortune 500 acquirer, the company had to rapidly replicate all of its contracts to ensure (i) every document was fully-executed (which meant getting an executive to sign a lot of paperwork) and (ii) scanned to PDF for transmission into a virtual data room for the buyer. A lot of weekend and evening administrative work was required merely to get the buyer basic contractual information.

Going International: Tips for Overcoming Multi-National Complexity

As a company grows and seeks additional markets for its solutions, it may consider going international and establishing operations in other countries. As complex as it is to comply with U.S. laws and taxes at the federal, state and local level, adding compliance with another country's laws and local jurisdiction is even more complicated. This is especially true if the company has little experience working in the foreign country, where language and terminology is often a barrier. No longer can a business rely solely on its local tax, accounting and legal advisors, as international operations typically necessitate local advisors who know local laws and practices, and who speak the relevant languages.

In a global marketplace, tech companies are going global much sooner in their business lifecycle than they ever have before.

Working with overseas customers or suppliers is usually not complex. The parties agree to a set of laws and currencies for their agreements with which both parties feel comfortable. Many international businesses are comfortable using the law and venue of one or more U.S. states, with State of New York in particular being popular for international contracts.

Once a company starts spending more time in-country and plan to hire personnel in-country, then the complexity really starts. Hiring employees locally means registering for local payroll tax obligations in that country, which means forming a company locally.

The laws of company formation in other countries different from that in the U.S. Some countries mandate a local resident being on the board of directors. Other countries mandate local ownership to establishing a bank account. Some countries have significantly more employee-friendly laws. Yet other countries have fewer rules and regulations. In nearly all cases, even in other English-speaking countries, the terminology, acronyms and processes are different from those in the U.S. Finding and working with competent local professionals (accounting, tax and legal) is essential.

Best practices dictate hiring a key, experienced executive in-country who can act as local management and take on key governance roles with respect to local taxing authorities, local banks and other key local stakeholders.

Typically, the new company will be wholly-owned and thus controlled by the parent company. By setting up a subsidiary rather than operating as a branch in a foreign country, the parent company's exposure to local tax risk and legal claims is minimized. Avoid the mistake of the parent company's founders or CEO owning the new local company. The subsidiary is an asset of the parent company, not of any specific one or group of employees or shareholders.

The new company will be obligated for various local taxes including payroll taxes, sales taxes (a.k.a. value added tax or goods & services tax in many jurisdictions), income taxes, etc. The local company will need a Board of directors, standardized contractual agreements in accordance with local laws and customs, etc.

Tax authorities for both the parent company and newly-formed subsidiary will need to ensure that neither location is a tax haven, where profits are stored intentionally away from taxing authorities. Thus, any international business must comply with transfer pricing regulations, where a sufficient profit is recognized in each jurisdiction, typically using an arms-length mandate.

Accounting and bookkeeping for the international business can occur locally or back at the corporate headquarters. Either way separate sets of books will need to be kept on different bases of accounting. For reporting purposes, the books may be consolidated into the parent company's functional currency. Other reports may be required for statutory purposes such as tax returns, in the local currency and unconsolidated. The bookkeeping for a multi-national company gets very complex, with multiple currencies and multiple sets of books.

Other corporate activities will need to be initiated, often for small tech companies by finance and admin personnel at headquarters. Ensure that all insurance coverages are applicable to the local jurisdiction. Often this means adding more insurance coverages for local operations, including a small local liabilities policy, a local employers liability policy and consideration of international travel policies especially when personnel will be traveling globally.

> *Story: A US-based communications technology service provider needed to hire personnel in Germany to meet customer needs. Nobody at headquarters spoke German or knew much about German employment obligations. So, they involved local German lawyers and accountants to establish a local company and begin the process of hiring personnel. During the lengthy process of establishing the local corporate entity, and unbeknownst to the local lawyers and accountants, the US parent company engaged with personnel in Germany as non-employee contractors, which is a common practice in the US. However, it was later learned that engaging contractors before a local legal entity is established is illegal in Germany, and faced the risk of noncompliance, fines and other ramifications.*

Liquidity Event: Preparing to Cash Out

The culmination of any technology company's tenure is an exit transaction whereby the company's ownership interests become liquid (a.k.a. a liquidity event). Typically, a liquidity event happens when the company's assets or stock is acquired by a third party, either a strategic acquirer or a financial buyer. Rarer are liquidity events through initial public offering (IPO) of the company's stock on a public stock exchange.

An acquisition typically starts with business discussions between the company's executive management team and the business managers at a potential strategic acquirer or financial buyer. Eventually, if the discussions proceed far enough, the parties may agree in writing on the general business terms of an acquisition. This written but non-binding agreement is called a Term Sheet or Letter of Intent. The purpose is to agree on high-level items which allows the buyer then to commence a detailed investigation of the business, called due diligence.

Due diligence typically involves a detailed and thorough investigation of all aspects of the company's business, including:

- Marketing dynamics: How big is the market that the company's products and services address? Is the market growing, and if so, how quickly? What competition exists (now and in the future)? Acquirers typically will pay more for a large market that's growing quickly where a company has a distinct advantage over competition.

- Executive leadership and personnel: Who are the key personnel? What key roles within the company need to be filled? What are the incentives to motivate and retain executives and key personnel? Some acquirers value a complete team, whereas others may only value a small subset of the acquirer's personnel.

- Intellectual property: If intellectual property is the basis for a company's product and strategic advantage, then an acquirer will seek to validate that the company properly owns it property, that it is not infringing on a third party's rights and will seek to understand what protections (such as patent filings) have taken place.

- Sales and marketing: A buyer that values a company's customer acquisition process will seek to understand what's working (and what's not working) in the sales and marketing process. Key sales and marketing performance metrics will be measured and possibly compared to baseline industry best practices.

- Accounting and taxes: Buyers will seek to understand the company's current and historical financial position and typically review historical financial statements, tax returns and audit reports. Any unusual accounting positions will need to be explained and all risks understood.

- Operational processes: Buyers will want to understand key processes involved in the company's operations. A buyer will want to understand what is working well and what is not working well. Key operational performance metrics will be measured and likely compared to baseline industry best practices.

- Corporate finance & risk management: Buyers will seek to understand outstanding company risks including measurements taken to mitigate those risks such as corporate insurance, employee medical benefits, etc.

- Legal: Expect that a buyer will want to review every contract (or at least every major contract) a company has entered with employees, customers and suppliers. A buyer's lawyers will scrutinize these contracts to uncover risks that may exist for the buyer that need to be addressed before or during the process of completing the transaction.

Due diligence can and should be a two-way endeavor whether they buyer is a strategic acquirer or a financial buyer. But typically, far more diligence is done by the buyer on the prospective seller since ultimately the Buyer is writing a sizable check to the Seller or its shareholders. Buyers will always learn new information in the due diligence process and will always find information they perceive to be negative about the business. Any surprises or negative findings can be used by the buyer to back out of the pending transaction and/or affect the terms of the transaction such as purchase price or timing of payments from buyer to seller.

Due diligence can take weeks or many months. The process can be extremely time-consuming and a massive distraction for the selling company's personnel and management team. The more organized and the better documented a company's processes, procedures and files are, the less painful the due diligence process will be.

Appointing a small team of dedicated personnel to manage the diligence process is a best practice. The goal of dedicating certain personnel is to minimize knowledge of the pending transaction within the company and to ensure that employees working on typical day-to-day activities aren't distracted with due diligence requests.

Upon completion of the due diligence process, the buyer's legal counsel will draft legal agreements documenting the transaction and addressing concerns and risks uncovered during due diligence. For sizable transactions, it's not uncommon for the legal paperwork to take months to draft and negotiate, results in hundreds if not thousands of pages of paperwork.

> *Story: Each buyer's (or investor's) due diligence will be a different based on the buyer's perceived risks and rewards of the transaction. Compare two different acquisitions, both for similar amounts of money and with a similar return on investment for shareholders.*
>
> *A digital media software company was acquired by a high-flying, IPO track software company which was growing extremely rapidly. The buyer had never*

previously made any acquisitions and its personnel leading the acquisition team had no experience with M&A. Their due diligence was light, driven primarily by their lawyers who naturally wanted to mitigate risks. And the project plan was loose, with little urgency or clarify on timing of tasks and deadlines. Business due diligence was almost non-existent, and the seller continually waited for the hard part of diligence, which never came.

A software infrastructure company was acquired by a Private Equity (PE) firm which had lots of experience with acquisitions and had a well-defined, step-by-step methodology for acquisitions to try to uncover all risks inherent in the business. The PE firm allocated more than $1 million to its legal, accounting, tax, management, HR and other consulting advisors to perform due diligence, which was extensive, intense and lengthy. The process was well-defined week by week and very structured.

At the end of the tedious process, if all goes to plan, is the financial reward for equity holders including the entrepreneur, shareholders and employees, who then start their next step anew with the Buyer.

Appendix I: Sample Chart of Accounts

This sample chart of accounts can be entered into the accounting system for tracking all company transactions.

Assets:

- Cash
- Accounts receivable
- Reserve for bad debts
- Other current assets
- Fixed assets
- Accumulated depreciation
- Other noncurrent assets

Liabilities & Equity:

- Accounts payable
- Accrued expenses
- Deferred revenue
- Current portion of debt
- Noncurrent portion of debt

Equity:

- Common stock
- Preferred stock
- Additional paid in capital
- Retained deficit

Revenue:

- License revenue
- Subscription revenue
- Set up fee revenue
- Professional services revenue
- Support revenue

Cost of Revenue

- Device depreciation
- Hosting costs
- Credit card processing fees

Employee related

- Employee bonus
- Commission
- Payroll tax
- Salaries
- Medical benefits
- Contract labor
- Recruiting fees
- Payroll fees

Depreciation & amort

- Depreciation

Equipment & software

- Equip & software maintenance
- Software expense

Facilities

- Rent
- Utilities

Insurance

- Directors & officers
- Liability
- Professional liability

Marketing

- Events
- Advertising
- Content automation
- Public relations
- Marketing agency
- Other content

Office expenses

- Postage & delivery

- Printing
- Office supplies

Other operating expenses

- Bad debt expense
- Bank fees
- Dues & subscriptions

Professional fees

- Accounting
- Consulting
- IT support
- Legal

Telecommunications

- Internet
- Local & long distance
- Wireless

Travel & entertainment

- Travel costs
- Meals & entertainment

Interest & other

- Interest income
- Interest expense
- Other income or expense

Taxes

- Federal income tax expense
- State income tax expense
- Other taxes

Appendix II: Sample Closing Checklist

This sample closing checklist can be used as a bullet-point or check-the-box list of actions taken each month to close the accounting books before issuing financial results to management and investors.

BALANCE SHEET

Assets

- Reconcile all cash accounts
    - Requires receipt of bank statement
    - Requires input of payroll journal entry
    - Print/save reconciliation upon completion
- Review accounts receivable (A/R) aging
    - Agree total A/R aging to balance sheet
    - Review invoices in A/R aging for accuracy
    - Review A/R reserve for adequacy
- Review other current assets and adjust as necessary
- Review fixed assets detail

- o Properly account for all acquired or disposed fixed assets
- o Prepare calculation of depreciation
- o Requires input of depreciation journal entry
- Review other non-current assets and adjust as necessary

<u>Liabilities</u>

- Review accounts payable (A/P) aging
  - o Agree total A/P aging to balance sheet
  - o Review invoices in A/P aging for accuracy
- Review notes payable current balance and adjust as necessary
- Review accrued expenses and adjust as necessary
  - o Accrued liabilities
  - o Accrued payroll
  - o Deferred rent
  - o Sales tax payable
- Reconcile deferred revenue accounts with sales entries
  - o Prepare analysis of deferred maintenance and unearned revenue
  - o Requires input of deferred revenue and unearned revenue journal entries
- Review capital lease – current portion and adjust as necessary
- Review capital lease – long term portion and adjust as necessary

<u>Equity</u>

- Review all equity accounts and adjust as necessary

- o Opening balance equity
- o Common stock
- o Additional paid in capital
- o Retained earnings

INCOME STATEMENT

<u>Gross Margin</u>

- Review revenue and cost of sales and adjust as necessary
- Review P&L by job
- Total revenue in P&L by job <u>plus</u> amortization of deferred revenue should equal total revenue per the P&L
- Ensure revenue is recorded according to company policy
  - o In proper period
  - o In proper account
  - o Matched to related cost of services if appropriate

<u>Operating Expenses</u>

- Review payroll costs and adjust as necessary
  - o Payroll costs should be similar to prior month, unless hiring & terminations have occurred
  - o Compare to budget
- Review travel expenses and adjust as necessary
- Review office expenses and adjust as necessary
- Review professional fees and adjust as necessary
- Review telephone expenses and adjust as necessary
- Review facilities costs and adjust as necessary
- Review interest income / expense and adjust as necessary

Appendix III: Key Performance Metrics

While every business differs, this list of sample key performance metrics can be used to analyze and understand the company's performance.

Financial KPI:

- Monthly Recurring Revenue (MRR): subscription or maintenance revenue that-will recur each month
- Days Sales Outstanding (DSO) trend: measures speed of collecting outstanding payment from customers
- Months to cash out trend: measures time until all company cash reserved are used up
- Monthly burn trend: measures company's monthly cash burn (both gross and net)

Marketing KPI:

- Number of leads generated by source trend: measures Marketing's ability to find new prospective customers

- Sales accepted leads: measures number of leads passed from Marketing to Sales for working to closure
- Established tech companies often develop a rigorous methodology of tracking and measuring leads as they progress from lead to nurturing to sales and won/lost.

Sales KPI:

- Bookings compared to plan (this month, this quarter to date, this year to date): measures ability to close deals with customers
- Revenue compared to plan (this month, this quarter to date, this year to date): bookings can hide timing of revenue recognition so measuring both bookings and revenue are key
- Average bookings per sales rep as a percentage of annual quota: measures average performance by each sales person relative to annual targets
- Traditional software and SaaS KPI's around lifetime value of a customer (LTV) and customer break-even (BE) are very relevant once a company is established and has a consistent history to measure customer attrition rates. But for a startup these are hard if not impossible to measure.

Customer success or implementation KPI:

- Count and MRR of customers not yet live trend: measures backlog of customers waiting to go live
- Average time to go live trend: measures how quickly the team can get a customer live once contract is signed

Account management or support KPI:

- Support or subscription retention rates: for recurring revenue businesses retention rate is perhaps the single most important metric
- Count of support tickets trends (open and closed): measures interaction with customers for support and issue tracking

Product development KPI:

- Count and percent of story points (for agile development environment): measures progress against goals for development team
- Bug count and trend: count of number of bugs in current product release

Appendix IV: Sample Offer Letter

This sample employee offer letter can be used as a template for making an offer of employment.

[Company letterhead]

January 1, 2018

John Doe
123 Main Street
New York, NY 10001

Dear John:

I am pleased to formally confirm our offer of employment as set forth below:

Start Date: It is anticipated that your start date will be January 16, 2018.

Position: You will be employed as Manager of Business Operations, based out of our offices in New York, NY, reporting to the Company's Chief Operating Officer.

Contingent: This offer of employment is contingent upon your satisfactory completion of a background investigation and verification that you can legally work in the United States, as well as your agreement to the terms of the employee handbook and the *Employment Covenants Agreement.*

Salary: In this position your base salary for the initial year of employment will be $100,000 per annum, which will be paid to you semi-monthly in arrears. This is an "exempt" role and you will not be eligible for overtime compensation.

Duties: Your primary responsibilities and key success criteria will be as set forth in the job description and as discussed with you. General responsibilities include: overall management of the Company's operations and personnel, coordinating with the executive management team, Board of Directors, investors and other stakeholder to ensure efficiency in the Company's business affairs.

Stock: Subject to approval of the Board of Directors, you will be granted options to purchase 10,000 shares of the Company's common stock, with a strike price and with terms and conditions set forth in the Stock Option Grant Certificate.

Hours: Your standard hours of work will be 8:30am to 5:30pm, and such hours as may from time to time be necessary to meet the needs of the company's business. This role does not require travel.

Health Plan: Company has a Healthcare plan in which you are eligible to participate, Details are available upon request. The Company covers 100% of your premiums and 50% of your direct dependents.

401K Plans: The Company has a 401K plan with a 4% match. Details are available upon request. You are eligible to participate subject to the terms of the plan which are the same for all employees.

Vacation: The Company provides 15 days of annual vacation, which is accrued pro rata on a calendar year basis. All vacation and holidays at Company are provided on a strict use it or lose it policy. Every employee is expected to plan ahead and coordinate with his or her manager to plan for proper utilization of vacation and holidays. Every effort will be made to be flexible during any given financial year but under no circumstances are vacation days or holidays carried over to future years.

Holidays: Company provides 8 days of public holidays as set forth in the Company's employee handbook.

Other: All employee benefits described in this letter are in summary only. Details of these plans can be found in the applicable plan documents, employee handbook, etc. and are subject to change by the company.

Termination: You are employed as an "At-Will" employee by the company. Either you or the company may terminate the employment relationship at any time, for any reason, or no reason. No inference shall be drawn from this offer of employment that you have any continuing right to be employed by the company and this offer of employment shall not restrict you or the company from terminating employment.

Expenses: The company will reimburse you for all reasonable business expenses wholly and exclusively incurred by you in the performance of your duties, provided you provide the company with the receipts or evidence of such expenses. Please be aware we will be controlling these expenses tightly. You will be expected to follow the company's expense policies.

Confidential: Details of your compensation and incentives are confidential and should not be discussed with other company employees or third parties.

Proprietary Information: By signing this letter you agree to respect the confidential and proprietary nature of Company products, clients, plans, documentation, company structure and records both during and for a period of one year following the end of your employment with Company. Attached please find an *Employment Covenants Agreement* for your signature, which is a condition of your employment.

Contingent Offer:	I understand and agree that this offer only becomes a binding agreement when this offer is signed by you and me in conjunction with the other documents provided as part of this offer of employment.
Expiration:	This offer of employment expires on January 5, 2018 if not signed by both parties such time.

I am very excited that you will be joining the Company. I look forward to working with you and am confident that your efforts and dedication will be a significant contribution to our success. Welcome aboard!

Sincerely,

Jane Smith

Jane Smith

Chief Operating Officer

I accept the terms and conditions of this offer and will begin employment on

Signed   Date

_____

John Doe

About the Author

Evan Rogoff headshot photo.

Evan Rogoff is a Certified Public Accountant (CPA) and a former Certified Turnaround Professional (CTP) with nearly 25 years of experience in corporate finance and entrepreneurship including nearly 20 years of experience working with rapidly-growing early-stage technology companies. He has started 5 businesses, including Rogoff Financial Services LLC to advise technology entrepreneurs on business, financial and operational strategy by serving as a fractional chief financial officer.

With his help, Evan's clients have:

- Raised over $150 million of capital in more than 3 dozen transactions, sourced from private equity, venture capital, angels, strategic partners, venture debt, banks and mezzanine debt providers
- Completed nearly 20 M&A transactions including 6 liquidity events which distributed $120 million to shareholders with returns as high as 20 times invested capital
- Expanded globally both for growth (overseas customer acquisition) and cost-savings (offshore personnel), establishing back-office functions in 8 countries across North America, Europe, Asia & Australia
- Balanced aggressive growth investments with need for profitability and cash flow to sustain ongoing operations for undercapitalized bootstrapped software company and maximize exit valuation
- Increased access to investors' capital by becoming a publicly traded company through a reverse merger into an existing shell

Technology companies that Evan has advised include businesses with various forms of revenue including software as a service (SaaS), perpetual license plus maintenance, technology-enabled managed services and professional services and have served various customers and clients including business-to-business (B2B), business-to-consumer (B2C), business-to-business-to-consumer (B2B2C).

These companies have been in various industries including: blockchain, artificial intelligence & machine learning, business intelligence & analytics, healthcare, cloud migration, digital media, cyber security, software development tools, telecommunication, digital marketing, mobile applications and human capital management (HCM), among others.

Other entrepreneurial businesses Evan has personally started or co-founded include:

- An innovative technology-enabled service driving new customer acquisition and loyalty for local restaurants
- A hybrid technology investment and accelerator firm for modernizing established entrepreneurial ventures
- A blockchain-based solution that assists with fulfillment of the promise of democratic institutions globally
- An internet-based developer of information products for entrepreneurs seeking to raise venture capital

Previously, Evan was part of the management team at an IPO candidate internet company which grew from start-up to $60 million and more than 300 employees in under 2 years. Before that, he was a manager in the corporate consulting practice at Arthur Andersen and part of the firm's audit team. Evan graduated with high distinction from the Ross School of Business at the University of Michigan. He is an active participant in the technology community and has been a speaker or presented to various industry groups. He served as President and a member of the Board of Trustees for the Technology Executives Roundtable and is a member of the American Institute of Certified Public Accountants.

Printed in the United States
By Bookmasters